6 MINUTE MORNING
MORNING

flat stomach

6 MINUTE MORNING

MORNING

flat stomach

SARA ROSE

Bath · New York · Singapore · Hong Kong · Cologne · Delhi · Melbourne

First published by Parragon in 2007

Parragon
Queen Street House
4 Queen Street
Bath BA1 1HE, UK

ISBN: 978-1-4075-1793-3

Printed in China

Created and produced by the Bridgewater Book Company Ltd.
Photography: Ian Parsons
Model: Lucinda Jarvis

The views expressed in this book are those of the author but they are general views only and readers are urged to consult a relevant and qualified specialist for individual advice in particular situations. Parragon hereby excludes all liability to the extent permitted by law for any errors or omissions in this book and for any loss, damage or expense (whether direct or indirect) suffered by a third party relying on any information contained in this book.

The Bridgewater Book Company would like to thank Getty Images for permission to reproduce copyright material on pages 7 (Barry Yee/Iconica) and 8 (Thomas Del Brase/Stone).

Caution
Please check with your doctor/therapist before attempting this workout, particularly if you are suffering from an injury, are pregnant or have just had a baby. It is recommended that new mothers wait at least six weeks post partum before participating in exercise (12 weeks if it was a Caesarean birth). If you feel any pain or discomfort at any point, please stop exercising immediately and seek medical advice.

CONTENTS

Most of us would love to have a flatter stomach but just can't face the thought of hours and hours of strenuous sit-ups. Well, the good news is you don't have to do this — the key to a flatter stomach is to exercise little and often. Just follow the quick and easy routines in this book and you'll have a flatter stomach within weeks.

Apart from the obvious benefit of improving your appearance, firming and toning up your stomach muscles is actually good for you. It will improve your posture and balance and increase your flexibility, helping to keep your body in good working order as you get older. Building muscle tone doesn't happen overnight, but the beauty of these short routines is that you won't become bored or burned out. Keep it up and you'll find that just 6 minutes a day really will make a difference.

How to use this book

This book has a series of easy exercises that are designed to fit into 6-minute programmes, enabling you to slot a workout into even your busiest day. Exercises are grouped into suggested programmes at the end of the book, but you can mix and match your own for even more variety.

Morning exercise

For most people exercising in the morning is best, when you are refreshed after a night's sleep. This is the time when your body is very receptive to exercise – since it tends to be done on an empty stomach, it forces you to use your fat reserves. As an added bonus, exercising at this time kick-starts your metabolism and helps keep you burning calories during the day.

Where to exercise and what you need

You don't need a home gym but it does help if you've got a clutter-free space that you can use regularly. If possible, try to exercise in front of a full-length mirror so that you can keep an eye on what you are doing. An exercise mat is a good idea for extra comfort, and you may wish to use a pillow to support your head and neck. Wear several layers of clothing to warm up your muscles as you start to exercise and strip off as you get warmer. Clothes should be loose and soft in a breathable fabric – shorts and a vest covered with jogging bottoms and a sweatshirt, for example, are ideal.

Food and fluids

Your stomach will naturally expand any time you eat or drink, but what you actually consume can directly affect the appearance of your stomach. You can keep bloating to a minimum by combining the following food and drink tips with a healthy eating plan. However, do be aware that if your stomach

has a noticeable wobble, you will have to reduce your body fat by changing your eating habits and building in some regular cardiovascular exercise. At first glance, drinking more water to help gain a flat stomach doesn't seem to make any sense – surely this will cause your belly to bloat? In fact, the opposite is true: water flushes out toxins and helps to curb your appetite. Drink at least eight glasses (two litres) of water a day (but don't drink large amounts before exercising or you'll put pressure on your bladder). To make sure you're drinking

enough water, check the colour of your urine – the paler it is, the better. If your body feels starved of water then it will hold on to what there is, which can lead to water retention and the appearance of bloating.

Body matters

Before you start a new toning routine, it helps to have an understanding of which muscles you need to work on to make your stomach appear flatter. There are four abdominal muscle groups, which form a natural corset around your middle. They support your lower back, protect your internal organs and enable you to bend, twist and sit up. The deepest of the abdominal muscles is the transversus abdominis, which wraps horizontally around your waist and keeps your lower back stable. The rectus abdominis runs

Diet for a flatter stomach

For a flatter stomach follow a healthy diet in addition to your exercise routines.

• Eat little and often and make sure you have a varied diet. Keep wheat products to a minimum as they cause bloating and wind.

• Choose a wide selection of fresh fruit and vegetables, and reduce the amount of saturated fat you consume.

• Sit down to eat and chew thoroughly. It takes 15 minutes for your brain to receive a message from your stomach telling you it's full, so if you eat too quickly you're liable to overeat because that crucial 'full' message will not have got to the brain in time.

• Don't eat too many starchy carbohydrates, such as rice, bread, potatoes and pasta. They're low in fibre (which means you will want to eat more, more often) and are stored mostly as fat.

• Say goodbye to fizzy drinks – even if they're 'diet' or caffeine-free, they still cause bloating because they're loaded with toxins.

• Avoid processed food and ready meals – laden with salt, sugar and chemicals, they upset your stomach's bacterial balance and cause bloating.

• Cut down on salt – it can encourage fluid retention.

• Biscuits, confectionery and cakes give an instant sugar rush rather than sustained energy levels, and promote cravings.

from the pubic bone to the bottom of the ribcage. This muscle enables your trunk to bend and is important for maintaining your posture. The external and internal obliques run up the sides of your body and enable you to bend to the side and twist your spine. The exercises in this book will work and strengthen all these muscles for a firmer, flatter, fabulously toned stomach.

Understanding terminology

Throughout this book various terminology is used. You will be asked to keep your spine in neutral. This means making sure your spine is in the right position when you are exercising your stomach area which will help you get much better results. Lie down on your back flat on the floor with your knees slightly bent and feet hip-width apart. Place your thumbs on your bottom ribs and your little fingers on the top of the hip bones. Draw these two points together by gently pulling your navel towards the floor to tighten your abdominal muscles.

Keep your back in contact with the floor – there should be a small space between the bottom of your back and the floor, but do not arch your spine. The trick is to let your back relax into its own natural position. Other terminology that you will come across in this book includes extension, which means to straighten a limb or spine. Bending a limb or spine is called flexion, and rotation means to turn the body on its axis.

Breathing

The correct way to breathe when exercising is to breathe in through your nose to prepare, breathe out through your mouth as you move into position and breathe in through your nose again when you are finishing the movement. Obviously, if the exercise takes time to do, you need to make sure you continue to breathe in and out regularly throughout. Breathing out as you move up will suck your abdominal muscles inward, tightening them up and working the deep muscles.

WARMING UP

Tempting though it is to save time by launching yourself straight into an exercise routine, if you don't warm up you are highly likely to injure yourself because cold muscles and joints are less flexible and more prone to strain. So the 6-minute routines do assume that you will have done your warming up beforehand.

Waist twist

It's important not to move your hips and knees during this exercise but do feel free to move your arms like a hula dancer if it helps you get into the right mood!

1 Stand up straight with your spine in neutral, and your knees slightly bent (soft, rather than 'locked'). Keep your feet hip-width apart and your hands resting on your hips. Make sure your spine is in the neutral position.

2 Tighten your abdominal muscles by pulling your navel back towards your spine.

3 Keeping your hips and knees still, rotate your shoulders and head to the right, then return to the centre.

4 Now twist to the left, rotating your head and shoulders and keeping your hips and knees still.

5 Repeat this exercise a further five times on each side.

1

3

Hip circles

This exercise will mobilize your lower abdominal muscles. Try to make sure that only your pelvis is rocking rather than your torso.

1 Stand up straight with your knees slightly bent, feet hip-width apart, hands resting on your hips.

2 Tighten your abdominal muscles by gently pulling your navel towards your spine. This movement should feel light and subtle – do not suck in your waist or hold your breath.

3 Gently rotate your pelvis to the right so that you are rotating in a full circle.

4 Repeat nine times to the right then circle ten times to the left.

Marching

This warming-up exercise will help to raise your body temperature and increase blood flow to the muscles. March on the spot for at least a minute, swinging your arms and gradually raising your knees higher as you go (but not so that you're goose-stepping). Make sure your breathing is deep and regular as you march. Once you feel warm, take the time to perform a few stretching exercises.

Forward bend

With this exercise, bend only as far as is comfortable – you don't have to touch your toes. Remember, you'll be able to stretch further as time goes by and you become more supple with exercise.

1 Stand up straight with your feet hip-width apart and your knees slightly bent rather than locked. Place your hands palm downward on the front of your thighs.

2 Tighten your abdominal muscles by gently pulling in your navel towards your backbone.

3 Slowly slide your hands down your legs towards your toes. Try not to over-arch your back.

Flatter stomach in a flash

A very simple way of making your stomach look flatter is simply to make sure your posture is correct. Good posture happens when your spine is in natural alignment rather than hunched or slouched. For an instant, more streamlined appearance, stand with your feet hip-width apart. Gently pull up through your legs, keeping your knees slightly bent. Lengthen your spine, pull in your stomach muscles and stand tall. Keep your shoulders down and relaxed so that your neck is as long as possible. Voilà – as if by magic, your stomach will look flatter!

1

4 Position yourself so you feel a stretch in the hamstrings at the back of your legs but don't stretch so far that it hurts.

5 Hold for a count of three then return to the centre.

6 Repeat four more times. Keep your breathing steady throughout.

WATCH POINT
Never stretch to the point of pain.

4

Side bends

Do not do this exercise quickly with your arms above your head because this will make it hard to control the movement.

1 Stand up straight with your feet hip-width apart and your knees slightly bent, your arms by your sides.

2 Tighten your abdominal muscles by gently pulling your navel towards your spine.

3 Keeping your back straight and without leaning forwards, slowly bend to one side from the waist so that your hand slides down the side of your leg. Straighten up again.

4 Repeat on the other side. Repeat four more times on both sides.

3

SEATED EXERCISES

These easy exercises can be performed when you're sitting at your desk or even when travelling. They're great for a quick tummy-toning session and for postural realignment. You'll need a straight-backed, sturdy chair – not one on castors.

Seated stomach workout

This tones and flattens your deep stomach muscle (transversus abdominis) and the one that runs down the front of your stomach (the rectus abdominis).

1 Sit forwards on a chair. Keep your feet flat on the floor, hip-width apart, with your knees over your ankles and your palms on your thighs.

2 Sit up straight. Tighten the abdominal muscles by gently pulling your navel in towards your spine. Hold for 10 seconds, then relax.

3 Rest for a count of three before doing any repetitions.

1

WATCH POINT
Remember to breathe regularly as you do this exercise – don't hold your breath because it will make your blood pressure rise, which can be dangerous when exercising.

Mind over matter

Get the most from your workout by focusing on what you are doing as you are exercising, and tell yourself how well you are doing. You can even use visualizations as you exercise to convince yourself that your body is becoming fitter and more toned!

Hip hitch

This strengthens the oblique abdominal muscles and helps to stabilize your pelvis. This exercise is perfectly safe to do during pregnancy.

1 Sit with good posture with your hands resting on your thighs. Extend upwards through your spine.

2 Lift one hip towards your ribs, hold for a count of ten then release. Repeat on the other side.

2

Sitting pretty

If you sit properly, not only will those concertina-rolls of flesh diminish but you'll be doing your back a favour, too! Sit up straight with both feet on the floor, hip-width apart, and with your knees directly over your feet (don't tuck your feet under the chair). Try not to slump backwards or forwards because you'll put pressure on your lower back. Avoid crossing your legs, because this pushes your spine out of alignment. Tighten your abdominal muscles by gently pulling in your navel towards your backbone. Relax your shoulders and gently squeeze your shoulder blades together to stop them from rounding. Make this second nature and you'll soon notice the difference – you'll be able to breathe more deeply because your abdomen won't be squashed.

SEATED EXERCISES

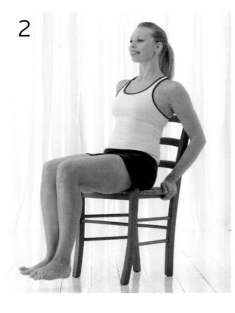

2

3

Seated knee lift

This seated exercise will work your rectus abdominis – the muscle that runs down the front of your stomach. Make sure your movements are controlled and flowing.

1 Sit on the edge of a chair with your knees bent and pressed together and your feet flat on the floor. Hold on to the sides of the chair, then tighten your stomach muscles.

2 Lean back slightly and lift your feet a few centimetres off the ground, keeping your knees bent and pressed together.

3 Slowly pull your knees in towards your chest and curl your upper body forwards. Then lower your feet to the floor. Rest for a count of three before you do any repetitions.

Controlling your movements

Make sure that all exercises are performed slowly, carefully, and with your full attention. You really do need to concentrate on what you're doing and think about how your body is responding to any exercise. If an action hurts or you do it quickly, then you're not doing it properly. Movements should flow in a gentle, controlled manner. This enables your muscles to stretch naturally.

WATCH POINT
Don't lean too far forwards or
you'll fall off the chair!

Spine rotation

This exercise gently mobilizes your spine, preparing it for harder exercises to come.

1 Sit forwards on a chair with your back straight and your hands resting on your thighs. Your knees should be over your ankles.

2 Tighten your abdominal muscles. Keeping your hips and knees forwards, slowly rotate your upper body to the left until you can put both hands on the back of the chair. Hold for a count of ten then return to the centre. Repeat the exercise, twisting to the right.

Don't exercise if...

- You are feeling unwell – your body will need all its strength to fight off any infection.
- You have an injury – you might make things worse.
- You have an ongoing medical condition or are on medication – consult with your doctor first.
- You've just had a big meal.
- You've been drinking alcohol.

WATCH POINT
Twist only as far as is comfortable.

PRONE EXERCISES

Exercising in this position means you are working against gravity, making your muscles work even harder. Remember to keep your elbows soft, not locked.

Belly tightener

This is also known as abdominal hollowing and helps to shorten the abdominal muscles, which is good for your posture and creates the appearance of a flatter stomach.

WATCH POINT
Pull up the abdomen by using your deep abdominal muscles, not by arching your spine.

1 Kneel down on all fours (the 'box' position) with your hands shoulder-width apart, your elbows slightly bent and your knees under your hips. Keep your head in line with the rest of your body and look down at the floor, making sure that your chin isn't tucked into your chest.

2 Relax your abdominal muscles then slowly draw in your navel towards your spine.

3 Hold the muscles in for a count of ten then slowly relax. Breathe slowly and steadily throughout this exercise.

Easy plank (tension hold)

Holding your body in a three-quarters plank shape strengthens the deep transverse muscles that cross the stomach area. Keeping your knees on the floor makes this exercise much easier than the traditional plank, which you can progress to when you feel ready.

1 Adopt a traditional press-up position but keep your knees on the floor and your feet in the air. Your fingers should point forwards, your elbows stay straight but not locked, your head should be in line with your body and your feet together. Keep your shoulder blades drawn into your back and make sure you don't dip in the middle or raise your bottom in the air.

2 Hold this position for a count of ten, breathing regularly throughout.

How to breathe properly

Breathing is something we all take for granted but most of us only ever use the top third of our lungs. Learn to breathe properly and it's probably the best thing you can do for your overall health, because oxygen nourishes and replenishes all your body's cells. Abdominal breathing is a technique that enables you to breathe more deeply. It uses the diaphragm, the sheet of muscle forming the top of the abdomen, to help the lungs inflate and deflate effortlessly. Breathe in slowly through your nose, and notice how the top of the abdomen rises as you do so. Hold the breath for a few seconds, then breathe out slowly through your mouth.

WATCH POINT
Avoid this exercise if you have shoulder problems. If you feel any strain in your back muscles, move your knees further apart.

1

PELVIC TILTS

These exercises tighten the abdominal muscles without putting any strain on your back. They're a simple way to tone and strengthen your abdominal area.

Simple pelvic tilt

This easy exercise is particularly good if you're trying to shape up post-pregnancy.

1 Lie on your back with your knees bent and feet flat on the floor, hip-width apart, and your spine in neutral. Rest your arms by your sides, palms facing the floor, and tighten your abdominal muscles.

2 Press your lower back down into the floor and gently tilt your pelvis so that the pubic bone rises, then tilt it back down.

3 Repeat several times, using a slow, steady rhythm.

Leg slide

Another easy exercise for tightening your stomach muscles.

1 Lie on your back with your knees bent, your feet flat on the floor and your arms by your sides, palms facing the floor. You can put a flat pillow or towel under your neck for support, if you like.

2 Tighten your abdominal muscles by gently pulling in your navel towards your backbone.

3 Gently tilt your pelvis so that the pelvic bone rises.

4 Raising the toes of one foot, breathe out while sliding your leg forwards as far as it will go, with your heel on the floor.

5 Hold for a count of three then return to the starting position and repeat using the other leg.

Lower abdominal raise

This is a harder exercise that will really work your deep abdominal muscles. If it seems easy then you're not doing it properly!

1 Lie on your back with your knees bent, feet flat on the floor and hip-width apart. Make sure your spine is in neutral. Keep your arms by your sides with the palms facing upwards.

2 Lift your legs into the air at an angle of 90 degrees to your body.

3 Tighten your abdominal muscles and slowly lower one foot to the floor then bring it back up again. Repeat this exercise using the other leg.

3

2

These exercises will tone the rectus abdominis muscle, which runs down the front of your stomach. As you lift your head and shoulders, this muscle contracts at both ends. Avoid these exercises if you have neck problems.

1

WATCH POINT
Never put your hands behind your neck when performing curls as you may tug on your neck muscles and strain your neck vertebrae.

Abdominal curl

Say farewell to sloppy sit-ups – a few properly executed curl-ups will work wonders in helping you achieve a flatter stomach.

1 Lie on your back with a firm, flat pillow or a small towel underneath your head. Keep your feet hip-width apart, parallel and firmly on the floor, and your knees bent. Rest your hands on your thighs.

2 Set your spine to the neutral position and tighten your abdominal muscles. Flex your spine to lift your head and shoulders gently about 30 degrees off the

floor. Your hands will slide up towards your knees as you curl. Keep your lower back in contact with the floor at all times. Slowly curl back down in a continuous movement.

To make this harder, put your hands across your chest as you curl. When this becomes easy, you can place your hands at the sides of your head to increase the resistance against which you are working.

2

Top tips for great curls

- Always keep your knees slightly bent (flexed).
- Breathe out as you curl up and breathe in on the return.
- Never hold your breath when exercising – blood pressure will rise and this can be dangerous.
- Perform all exercises in a slow, controlled manner.
- Don't put your hands behind your neck because you are likely to tug on the neck vertebrae.

Moving curl

This exercise gives your rectus abdominis an intensive workout by repeating the hardest part of the abdominal curl.

1 Lie on your back with your feet flat on the floor, knees bent and your arms by your sides (palms facing downwards). Keep your spine in neutral.

2 Tighten your abdominal muscles. Start curling up by lifting your head and shoulder blades off the floor while reaching forwards with your arms.

3 Curl up about 30 degrees off the floor. Then extend your arms and lift and lower yourself just a few centimetres up and down from this position.

4 Repeat several times, then lower.

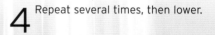

OBLIQUE CURLS

Twisting curls work your rectus abdominis muscles and the obliques, the muscles that give definition to the waist. These exercises will tighten your stomach muscles and trim your waist.

Basic oblique curl

1 Lie on your back with your knees bent, feet flat on the floor and hip-width apart. Put your hands by your temples at the sides of your head. Lift your left leg and rest the ankle of that leg across your right thigh – this will turn your supported left leg out slightly. Keep your spine in neutral and tighten your abdominal muscles.

2 Curl up, rotating your trunk to the left and breathing out as you do so. Your right elbow should be moving towards your left knee. Keep your left side in contact with the floor to help support your back.

3 Curl back down again, breathing in as you do so.

4 Repeat this exercise to the other side using the other leg.

1

2

Slightly harder oblique curl

1 Lie on your back with your spine in neutral, your knees bent and your feet flat on the floor, hip-width apart. Put your right hand by your temple at the side of your head. Lift your left leg and rest the ankle of that leg on your right knee. Wrap your left hand around the inside of your left thigh and press your thigh outwards.

2 Breathe in and tighten your abdominal muscles. Breathe out as you curl up and across to bring your right elbow towards your left knee.

3 Curl back down again, breathing in as you do so, then cross over your right leg and work the other side.

Neck support

Many people complain of neck pain when starting abdominal work. This is usually because you are using the neck muscles rather than the abdominal muscles to lift your head and shoulders. One solution is to place a towel behind your head and hold both ends taut so it supports your neck while you are curling up.

WATCH POINT
Avoid this exercise if you have neck problems.

1

2

Reverse curls give a good workout to the transversus abdominis, the deepest abdominal muscle that wraps around your waist like a corset, and the rectus abdominis, the stomach muscle that's responsible for the six-pack look.

Reverse curl

Remember not to arch your back as you do this exercise.

1 Lie on your back with your spine in neutral, your arms by your sides, palms facing downwards. Tuck your knees in towards your stomach and cross your ankles.

2 Tighten your abdominal muscles by gently pulling your navel in towards your spine.

3 Roll your knees towards your chest and then lower them down again.

WATCH POINT
Remember to breathe regularly throughout.

How muscles work

Here's the science: muscles are made up of millions of tiny protein filaments that relax and contract to produce movement. Most muscles are attached to bones by tendons and are consciously controlled by your brain. Electrical signals from the brain travel via nerves to the muscles, causing the cells within the muscle to contract. Movement happens when muscles pull on tendons, which move the bones at the joints. Muscles work in pairs, enabling bones to move in two directions, and most movements require the use of several muscle groups.

Slightly harder reverse curl

1 Lie on your back with your spine in neutral. You can keep your hands by the sides of your head or rest your arms by your sides with the palms facing downwards. Keep your legs up vertically with the knees bent and your ankles crossed over. Tighten your abdominal muscles.

2 Tilt your pelvis forwards so that your bottom lifts off the floor, keeping your legs still as you do so. Lower your pelvis to the start position.

Ditch the sit-ups

Never do full sit-ups – curling is much safer and more effective. To exercise a muscle properly, it has to be worked as a prime mover – in other words, the main muscle that contracts to move a joint. In a sit-up, the abdominals are the prime movers for only the first 30 degrees of movement, after which the remainder of the movement relies on the hip flexor muscles, which are attached to the lower back. Since this is not a rigid attachment point but a flexible column, strong tension in the hip flexor muscles can put enormous strain on your lower back.

2

CHALLENGING CURLS

Your stomach muscles will work really hard with these exercises but they're not for absolute beginners. You should wait until you've toned your abdominal muscles with a few weeks' worth of routines before you attempt these exercises.

Side reach

The small, controlled movements in this exercise work your stomach muscles even harder.

1 Lie on your back with your spine in neutral, your knees bent, feet flat on the floor, hip-width apart, and palms down and by your sides. Tighten your abdominal muscles.

2 Lift your head and shoulders off the floor to an angle of 30 degrees. Hold this position and reach out with your right hand towards your right calf.

3 Gently move back and forth ten times, then curl back down again. Remember to breathe regularly throughout.

4 Now repeat this exercise, reaching out with the left hand towards the left calf. Gradually build up the number of reaches you can do.

4

2

Long-arm curl

You will need to be able to perform basic curls with ease before you attempt this.

1 Lie on your back with your spine in neutral, your knees bent, feet hip-width apart and flat on the floor. Raise both arms above your head.

2 Engage your abdominal muscles, and begin to slowly curl your head and shoulders off the floor. Keep your arms in line with your ears throughout.

3 Continue the movement using your abdominal muscles, until your upper back is raised at an angle of 30 degrees.

4 Hold for a count of two then slowly lower yourself back down, breathing in as you do so.

'Hundreds'

This is a Pilates exercise – a system of exercise much favoured by dancers – that tones the whole abdominal area. For a harder version, lift your legs off the floor and extend them (still keeping your knees slightly bent).

1 Lie on your back with your hands by your sides, hovering above the ground, palms facing downwards. Keep your knees slightly bent and your feet on the floor throughout. Your spine should be in neutral. Tighten your abdominal muscles.

2 Curl your head and shoulders off the floor but keep your lower back in contact with the floor throughout. In this position, move your arms up and down, slowly breathing in and out as you do so. Breathe in for five flaps and out for five.

Double-leg push-out

This exercise works the transverse (deep) abdominal muscles as you extend your legs.

1 Sit on the floor with your knees bent and your feet parallel, toes just touching the floor but your heels lifted off it.

2 Lean back slightly and support yourself by placing your hands behind you, palms downwards. Tighten your abdominal muscles.

3 Extend both legs in front of you but do not straighten your legs completely. Bring them back to the starting position.

Dressing for a flatter stomach

Find practical solutions to help you look your best and feel positive about the way you look right now. Don't try to hide your lumps and bumps under baggy tops and elastic-waisted jogging bottoms – this just draws attention to the fact that you've got something to hide! Buy clothes that fit properly: stomach-skimming vests really don't look nice on fuller figures. Finally, keep high heels for special occasions only. Heels throw your body weight forwards, ruining your posture.

Leg kick-up

This is a tough one and only for when you can perform curls with ease.

1 Lie on your back with your spine in neutral and your arms stretched out behind your head. Bend your right knee and keep your right foot flat on the floor but keep your left leg extended a little with the knee slightly bent.

2 Tighten your abdominal muscles by gently pulling your navel in towards your spine. Slowly curl your shoulders off the floor and bring your left leg up towards your chest, raising your arms as you lift. Release down to the floor and repeat on the other side.

Keeping up your motivation

All too often people start a new exercise regime burning with enthusiasm, only for it to peter out very quickly to the point when they can't be bothered to do anything at all. When you start your toning programme, be realistic about how and when you can do it. You do need to set aside a regular slot for your 6-minute routine so it becomes a natural and automatic part of your everyday routine, just like brushing your teeth. But if you do miss several days, don't get disheartened and give up – a little exercise even on a very irregular basis is still better than nothing at all!

WATCH POINT
Make sure you keep your chin off your chest.

1

2

WATCH POINT
Don't do this exercise
if you have back problems.

Pillow roll

This exercise tones and strengthens your obliques and is a safe way to mobilize your spine. Your shoulders and arms should stay on the floor throughout but you may find to begin with that the opposite arm and shoulder come up slightly.

1 Lie on your back on the floor with your arms out to the sides at shoulder height, palms flat on the floor. Keep your knees bent. Your feet should be touching and off the floor but to make this exercise easier you can keep your feet on the floor throughout if necessary.

2 Put a cushion or pillow between your knees – this will make you keep your knees together, which is important for this exercise.

3 Tighten your abdominal muscles and remember to breathe normally – do not hold your breath.

4 Slowly bend your legs towards the floor on your right side, rolling your head to the left as you do so. Feel each part of your body peel up as you move – your buttocks, then hips, then waist and ribs. Keep going until your right knee and foot are touching the floor with your left leg lying on top.

5 Move your knees and head back to the central position.

6 Repeat this exercise on the other side with your legs towards the left side and your head to the right.

Toe touch

This exercise helps to flatten the deep transverse muscles.

1 Lie on your back on the floor with your spine in neutral, your knees over your hips and your feet raised, parallel to the floor.

2 Tighten your abdominal muscles by gently pulling in your navel towards your backbone – do not suck in your waist or hold your breath.

3 Slowly lower one leg until your toes touch the floor. Move your leg back to the starting position, then repeat on the other side.

Bin the broom handle

A long-practised exercise is to place a pole or broom handle across your shoulders and, with your arms stretched along it, twist your body vigorously from side to side in the hope that this will help to whittle your waist. This sort of exercise actually does more harm than good because it produces a ballistic twisting movement around the spine (the axis of rotation). Not only are you likely to damage your obliques, you may also stretch and tear tiny spinal ligaments. In addition, the weight of your upper body pressing down exerts extreme force on your spinal column – slipped disc, anyone? Ouch!

1

3

Leg lift

This exercise helps to develop the deep (transverse) abdominal muscles as well as working your hamstrings (the muscles at the back of your thighs).

1 Lie on your back with your arms by your sides, palms facing downwards. Keep your knees bent and feet hip-width apart, flat on the floor. Tighten your abdominal muscles.

2 Raise your left leg to the ceiling, keeping your knee slightly bent, then lower it. Then raise your right leg and lower it in the same way.

Setting the pace

It's important to work at the right intensity if you're toning up – put in too little effort and you won't notice much difference; throw yourself into the exercises and you may hurt yourself. The aim of a toning programme is to make your muscles work harder, either by increasing the time you exercise or by increasing the intensity of your workout. Your muscles will start to become tired during the last repetitions and you may feel a burning sensation in the area you're working but this is normal and will pass as soon as you rest. Muscle soreness and stiffness is highly likely in the beginning, particularly if you're new to exercise, but if you can hardly move then you've overdone it. Rest up for a day or so and start again at a reduced intensity.

2

3

Leg stretch

This exercise tests your balance as well as working your stomach muscles.

1 Lie on your back on the floor with your feet hip-width apart and your knees bent. Breathe in to prepare.

2 As you breathe out, tighten your abdominal muscles and pull one knee at a time up to your chest.

4

3 Breathe in and grasp your left knee with both hands.

4 Breathe out and slowly straighten your right leg up to the ceiling, keeping your back and your shoulders on the floor at all times.

5 Breathe in and bend the right leg back into your chest. Repeat the exercise with the other leg.

5

WATCH POINT
If you feel your back arching, raise your extended leg higher to flatten it out.

FURTHER OBLIQUES

Both these exercises are great waist-whittlers but you may find them too hard if you're a beginner – you should be able to do these after a few weeks of stomach-toning exercise.

1

2

3

Side lift

This exercise works the obliques and reinforces your body's natural alignment. Make sure you don't use the supporting arm to push yourself up – the movement is controlled by the stomach muscles.

1 Lie on your side in a straight line. Extend your lower arm above your head in line with your body. Bend your top arm in front to support you – your hand should be in line with your chest.

2 Tighten your abdominal muscles, then lift both legs together off the floor.

3 Now raise your upper leg higher, keeping it parallel with the bottom leg.

4 Hold for a count of two then lower the top leg to the bottom leg.

5 Lower both legs slowly to the floor. Repeat on the other side of your body.

Don't rest too much
Don't stop for more than a minute between exercises. Shorter recovery periods result in better muscles all round and improved muscle endurance. Keep it up!

WATCH POINT
Don't arch your back.

Repetitions

Muscle-building exercises are done as a series of repetitions. One repetition equals one exercise. A set is a group of repetitions and usually consists of anything between 6 and 12 repetitions. To build strength and endurance you will be asked to repeat the same exercise again and again. The aim is to work until your muscles feel tired, and over time this will strengthen them so that they can work harder.

Bicycle

This is a tough exercise that really works the obliques – and you'll need strong abdominal muscles to do this exercise properly. Make sure your shoulders are off the floor throughout.

1 Lie on your back with your knees bent and your hands cradling the sides of your head for support.

2 Tighten your abdominal muscles and curl up about 30 degrees off the floor.

3 Slowly bring your right knee to your chest. Straighten your left leg out without letting it touch the floor.

4 Drop your right leg and repeat with your left leg.

To make this exercise even harder, as you bring your knee to your chest, twist your torso towards your knee so that the opposite elbow touches it.

WATCH POINT
Don't bring your elbows together – keep them open.

STRETCHES

Your exercise routine concentrates on working your abdominal muscles hard to shorten them but it's important to remember that these muscles also need to be stretched in order to keep your body supple and injury-free.

WATCH POINT
Stretch only as far as is comfortable otherwise you may strain your back muscles.

Cobra stretch

This modified yoga position is excellent for stretching your stomach muscles.

1 Lie on your front on the floor and put your hands underneath your shoulders.

2 Breathe in to prepare, then gently push your arms up until they are straight but your elbows are not locked. This will lift your head and chest upwards and you will feel a stretch in your abdominal muscles. Your hips should stay in contact with the floor throughout.

3 Hold for a count of ten then lower yourself back to the ground.

Lying waist stretch

1 Lie on the floor on your back with your knees bent and your feet flat on the floor. Keep your arms stretched out to either side. Breathe in to prepare.

2 Breathe out and pull in your abdominal muscles. Slowly bend both knees to the left while turning your head to the right.

3 Hold for a count of ten then return to the starting position. Repeat, bending your knees to the other side.

Sitting body twister

1 Sit on the floor with your legs straight out in front of you. Bend your left leg and cross it over your right knee.

2 Gently rotate your trunk and head towards your right as far as is comfortable, keeping your buttocks on the floor throughout.

3 Hold for a count of ten then release and return to the starting position. Repeat on the other side.

WATCH POINT
Stretch only as far as is comfortable.

1

2

STRETCHES

Side stretch

1 Kneel on your left knee and straighten your right leg out to the side.

2 Put your left hand on the floor and bring your right arm over your head until you feel a stretch in your side.

3 Hold for a count of ten then return to the starting position. Repeat on the other side of the body.

Top tips for super stretching

- Only stretch warm muscles.
- Slowly ease the muscle into position.
- Do not bounce into position.
- Never overstretch – mild discomfort is acceptable but if it hurts, you should stop.
- Don't hold your breath – breathing freely will enable blood to flow to the muscles.

2

Standing waist stretch

1 Stand with your legs fairly wide apart, knees soft. Turn your right foot outwards and bend the knee of the right leg so that you can lunge to that side. Keep your left leg straight with the foot flat on the floor and pointing forwards. Rest your right palm on your right thigh to support your body weight.

2 Lift your left arm above your head and lean towards your right side. Hold for a count of ten. Repeat on the other side.

1

2

WATCH POINT
Don't lean too far over – you should feel a stretch in your obliques but it shouldn't hurt.

Just as important as warming up before exercising is cooling down afterwards. Help your body return to normal in a gentle way by taking the time to perform cooling-down stretches at the end of an exercise session. As well as helping to prevent dizziness and a sudden drop in body temperature (which can make you feel unwell), cooling down realigns working muscles to their normal position to avoid post-exercise tightness and stiffness. Cooling down also helps you to relax and gives you a few quiet moments to yourself before carrying on with the rest of your day. Cooling-down stretches can be held for longer than 10 seconds because the muscles are warm.

Leg lift and cross

1 Lie on your back with your legs out straight and your arms stretched out to the sides.

2 Breathe in to prepare, and tighten your abdominal muscles. Lift your right leg up to the ceiling as you breathe out, and flex your foot.

3 Using your abdominal muscles to control the movement, lower your leg across your body over to the right side until the foot touches the floor.

4 Hold for a count of 20 then slowly return to the starting position. Repeat on the other side.

WATCH POINT
If you can't take your foot all the way to the floor, bend your arm up to meet your foot and rest the foot on your hand.

3

2

Lying full body stretch

1 Lie flat on your back and relax. Breathe in and extend your arms outwards and backwards so that they meet behind your head. Try to keep your arms on the floor throughout the movement but if this isn't possible just keep them as low as possible.

2 Gently stretch out your body from your fingertips to your toes. Your lower back may lift from the floor a little.

3 Hold for a count of 20 then slowly release, bring your arms back down to your sides and relax.

WATCH POINT
If you have any back problems, keep your knees bent slightly throughout. Also, be aware that if you are unused to stretching you may feel tightness in your shoulders or cramp in your feet – in which case, relax. You will be able to hold this stretch for longer with practice.

1

2

TWO-WEEK PLAN

Here's a simple two-week plan for you to follow. Although these exercises are grouped into 6-minute sessions, if you're new to exercise please don't feel you have to start off doing the whole routine – you can build up the amount of time you spend and the types of exercises you do. You can also make up your own routines. The exercises in this book will tone your stomach muscles quickly, but be aware that they are not for fitness or weight loss.

Do what feels right for you

The exercise programme outlined on these pages suggests that you do one 6-minute routine every day. However, if you do not usually exercise regularly it is a good idea to start off by doing the routines every other day to give your body time to recover. Similarly, if you experience stiffness or pain the day after exercising, it is important to take a break that day. Each routine should take 6 minutes to do, but this may vary depending on the amount of reps you do. The workouts gradually build in intensity, so you may wish to repeat the first week's routine in subsequent weeks until you feel ready to incorporate the second week's more challenging schedule into your fortnightly programme.

Day 1

Belly tightener: *2-4 reps* **p18**
Simple pelvic tilt: *1 set (8-12 reps)* **p20**
Abdominal curl: *1 set (6 reps)* **p22**
Pillow roll: *1 set (6 reps) on each side* **p32**
Cobra stretch **p38**
Lying waist stretch **p38**

Day 2

Seated stomach workout: *2-4 reps* **p14**
Seated knee lift: *1 set (6 reps)* **p16**
Hip hitch: *5 reps on each side* **p15**
Easy plank: *2 reps* **p19**
Side stretch **p40**
Cobra stretch **p38**

Day 3

Leg slide: *1 set (10 reps) for each leg* **p20**
Toe touch: *1 set (6-8 reps)* **p33**
Reverse curl: *1 set (6-8 reps)* **p26**
Basic oblique curl: *1 set (6-8 reps)* **p24**
Side stretch **p40**
Sitting body twister **p39**

Day 4

Abdominal curl: *1 set (6-8 reps)* **p22**
Leg stretch: *1 set (10 reps) for each leg* **p35**
Double-leg push-out: *1 set (10 reps)* **p30**
Side lift: *2-4 reps on each side* **p36**
Standing waist stretch **p41**

Day 5

Leg slide: *1 set (10 reps) for each leg* **p20**
Leg lift: *1 set (10 reps) for each leg* **p34**
'Hundreds': *5 reps* **p29**
Side reach: *2 reps on each side* **p28**
Cobra stretch **p38**
Standing waist stretch **p41**

Day 6

Belly tightener: *4 reps* **p18**
Lower abdominal raise:
   1 set (6-8 reps) **p21**
Reverse curl: *1 set (6-8 reps)* **p26**
Pillow roll: *1 set (6-10 reps)*
   on each side **p32**
Sitting body twister **p39**

Day 7

Easy plank: *2-4 reps* **p19**
Simple pelvic tilt:
   2 sets (16-20 reps) **p20**
Moving curl: *2-4 reps* **p23**
Toe touch:
   1 set (6-8 reps) for each leg **p33**
Leg stretch:
   1 set (10 reps) for each leg **p35**
Cobra stretch **p38**

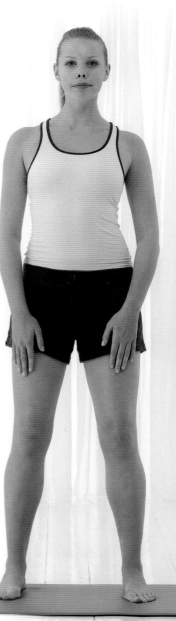

Day 8

Belly tightener: *4 reps* **p18**
Simple pelvic tilt: *2 sets (16-20 reps)* **p20**
Abdominal curl: *1 set (8-12 reps)* **p22**
Basic oblique curl: *1 set (8-12 reps)*
   on each side **p24**
Lying waist stretch **p38**
Sitting body twister **p39**

Day 9

Seated stomach workout: *4 reps* **p14**
Seated knee lift: *1 set (6-8 reps)* **p16**
Slightly harder oblique curl:
   1 set (8-10 reps) on each side **p25**
Cobra stretch **p38**
Side stretch **p40**

Day 10

Belly tightener: *4 reps* **p18**
Moving curl: *1-2 sets (6-20 reps)* **p23**
Long-arm curl: *1 set (6-8 reps)*
   on each side **p29**
'Hundreds': *1 set (6-10 reps)* **p29**
Cobra stretch **p38**
Sitting body twister **p39**

Day 11

Easy plank: *4 reps* **p19**
Slightly harder reverse curl:
   1-2 sets (10-20 reps) **p27**
Leg kick-up: *1 set (6-10 reps)*
   on each side **p31**
Side lift: *4-6 reps on each side* **p36**
Side stretch **p40**
Standing waist stretch **p41**

Day 12

Lower abdominal raise: *1 set (6-8 reps)* **p21**

Abdominal curl: *2 sets (12-20 reps)* **p22**

Long-arm curl: *1-2 sets (10-20 reps)* **p29**

Bicycle: *1 set (6-10 reps) on each leg* **p37**

Cobra stretch **p38**

Lying waist stretch **p38**

Day 13

Belly tightener (4 reps) **p18**

Slightly harder oblique curl:

   1 set (6-10 reps) on each side **p25**

Side reach: *1 set (6-10 reps)*

   on each side **p28**

Leg kick-up: *1 set (10 reps)*

   on each leg **p31**

Sitting body twister **p39**

Taking it further

These routines are fine for toning and sculpting your stomach but if you want to get fit then you'll have to include some activity that raises your heartbeat for at least 15 minutes at a time. Swimming, cycling, fast walking and running are all straightforward options but you could do an exercise class or take up a sport such as tennis if you like — just keep moving and try a variety of activities.

Making the most of your workout

- Always warm up before you begin.
- Think about what you are trying to achieve and be aware of how your body feels as you move.
- Remember to tighten your abdominal muscles.
- Keep your spine in neutral.
- Breathe in to prepare and breathe out as you move into position.
- Move slowly and gracefully.
- Cool down at the end to relax and bring your body back to normal.

Day 14

Moving curl: *1-2 sets (10-20 reps)* **p23**

Reverse curl: *1-2 sets (10-20 reps)* **p26**

Double-leg push-out:

   1-2 sets (10-20 reps) **p30**

Toe touch: *1 set (6-10 reps)*

   on each leg **p33**

Side lift: *1 set (6-8 reps) on each side* **p36**

INDEX